BROKEN

FOR PURPOSE

Yielding Vessel

ISBN 979-8-88616-099-4 (paperback)
ISBN 979-8-88616-636-1 (hardcover)
ISBN 979-8-88616-100-7 (digital)

Christian Faith Publishing
832 Park Avenue
Meadville, PA 16335
www.christianfaithpublishing.com

Unless otherwise noted, all scripture references are from the King James Version (KJV).

Printed in the United States of America

Contents

Preface

For all intended aim and design, the scope of this journey is to appoint and proclaim a triumphant end. *Broken for Purpose* was birthed out of a yielding vessel whom God has allowed suffering to purpose it!

On January 3, 2016, Bishop James E. Holloway Sr. spoke a prophetic event that positioned my life. A symbolic wave began to charge the atmosphere. Bishop asked us to take our hand and push the past behind. We could hear the profound sound of removal of the weights that so easily beset us as they began to drop off.

> Wherefore seeing we also are compassed about with so great a cloud of witnesses, let us lay aside every weight, and the sin which doth so easily beset us, and let us run with patience the race that is set before us. (Hebrews 12:1)

We have to lay aside every weight that is hindering our Christian progress.

Along with the prophetic sound there comes a symbol of healing. Our first lady, Linda D. Holloway, is a Repairer of the Breach, a title that represents the idea of a great laborer for the wounded.

> And they that shall be of thee shall build the old waste places; thou shalt raise up a foundations of many generations; and thou shalt be called, the repairer of the breach, the restorer of the paths to dwell in. (Isaiah 58:12)

The same day, January 3, 2016, the number three was given the meaning of completeness the finality. Three appears in measurements of time: three days, three months, or years. Three gives the idea of the beginning, the middle, and the end. There is strength in numbers. Our Scripture was taken from Philippians chapter 3 verses 1, 2, 5, and 7:

> Finally, my brethren, rejoice in the Lord. To write the same things to you, to me indeed is not grievous, but for you it is *safe* [my italics]. Let your happiness be in the Lord... Beware of dogs, beware of evil workers, beware of the concision... Circumcised the eighth day, of the stock of Israel, of the tribe of Benjamin, an Hebrew of the Hebrews; as touching the law, a Pharisee... But what things were gain to me, those I counted loss for Christ.

In Christ we are *safe*!

Now begins the journey: broken for purpose.

The birthing place of *Broken for Purpose* came from a group of women I was working with in 2002. God already had a Bible study group established called "Branches," according to John 15:5 ("I am the vine, yea are the Branches: he that abideth in me, and I in him, the same bringeth forth much fruit: for without me ye can do nothing"). Jesus is the true vine! As we abide in the Lord and He in us, we will bring forth good fruit! In a huge corporation, we met every Monday and Wednesday. The women branched off to meet the needs of just women while staying with Branches. We would gather monthly and pour out to the Lord. We would pray for each other, dance, sing, and create music with a saxophonist; whatever talent and gift the Lord gave we would openly give back to each other.

The Spirit of the Lord gave one woman the scripture Jeremiah 29:11: "For I know the thoughts that I think toward you, saith the LORD, thoughts of peace, and not of evil, to give you an expected end."

The Spirit of the Lord spoke to me and said, "I put in you a spirit to restore others unto me!"

God gives a ninefold restoration plan of what the Lord will think and do concerning our expected end:

1. He *promises* He will visit us.
2. He will *perform* His word to us.
3. He will cause us to return to our own land again.
4. He has *good thoughts toward us, thoughts of peace and not evil, to give us an expected end.*
5. You will call upon the LORD and will pray to Him, and He will *hear* you.
6. You will seek Him and find Him when you *search* for Him with all your *heart.*
7. He will be fond of you.
8. He will turn away all your captivity and will gather you from all nations where He has driven you.
9. He will bring you again into a place whence He caused you to be carried away.

God was clearly saying, "This time your deliverance will not depend upon you or false things but upon My mercy, thoughts, and purpose!"

The thoughts and expected end of the Lord's heart will be to your generation.

God's future for us will be of love and hope, followed by restoration.

The meaning of *restoration* is the action of returning to a place or condition that was always meant for you by the Lord. A place of repair, mending, refurbishing, reconditioning, rehabilitation, rebuilding, reconstruction, overhaul, redevelopment, renovation, and reinstatement.

The word of *restoration* was being put into action by the Lord. He was increasing what had already been planted and watered.

I would get up every morning at the 3:00 a.m. watch, and the Lord would birth a dance in me. I had not danced in twenty years.

The Spirit spoke, "You used to dance, learning tap and ballet. Now dance for Me." I pondered because I could not even imagine what that would look like. But with the fragrance from the Lord, it would look like purpose!

Everyone was asleep; the day was already prepared for and complete. I felt an awakening in the Spirit. I repented, worshiped, read, and danced for seven months before I went forth every morning at the 3:00 a.m. watch.

The Spirit of the Lord gave me the unction to dance, and a song from Smokie Norful, "I Need You Now," came to mind.

My experience of the song deepened each time I heard it. My tears got stronger. I was in the middle of a great test, and it was God and me. He met me at 3:00 a.m. every morning, teaching me, covering me, preparing me, and restoring me. Every word of that song became real for me!

We were at work, and it was time for the women to get together monthly. One of my spiritual sisters said, "It's time for you to come forth." I heard her, but I heard God through her. The voice of God allows you to obey. I knew it was time to minister in dance for the Lord. The women wept and cried and repented and there began our restoration!

Rough and Rutted Brings Repentance

The direction of an uneven, rough, and rutted path takes us to a place where deep tracks made by repeated regret and remorse for wrongdoings meet. No deposit, no return. True repentance is being in a place of returning from self to God. Our daily walk should be a constant endeavor for a persistent, holy life.

> As I journeyed through a place, being in some turbulent waters,
> Walking through fire and the flood,
> Being served divorce papers on my job, my boss read the serving,
> Openly humiliated, lied on,
> Loss of child,
> Information of discord tried to destroy my character,
> I was overwhelmed!
> I heard the Lord say, "When your heart is overwhelmed, I will take you to a rock higher than you, higher than your circumstance."
> Then the man of wisdom said, "Daughter, humility before honor!"
> I put my head down, I pushed my mute button down to close my mouth

And I thought of all that I had already endured. I said, "Yes, sir."

I was about to enter into deep waters.
Isaiah 43:2 says,

> When thou passest through the waters, I will be with thee; and through the rivers they shall not overflow thee; when thou walkest through the fire, thou shalt not be burned; neither shall the flame kindle upon thee.

Pass through the waters and the Lord will be with thee; pass through without the rivers overflowing thee; pass through without being burned or smelling like smoke!

Even the prophet Elijah had to pass through the waters. God's people were worshiping gods in Israel under the rulership of King Ahab. Elijah gave a word to King Ahab of Israel when he saw all the Baal (idol) worship in the land. He went straight to King Ahab and said, "As the Lord, the God of Israel, lives, whom I serve, there will neither be dew nor rain in the next few years, except at my word!" You can imagine that the people threatened Elijah's life. The drought came just as Elijah said it would. God told Elijah to go hide by the brook and get fed.

As we pass through the waters, God gives direction, as it says in 1 Kings 17:3, "Get thee hence, and turn thee eastward, and hide thyself by the brook Cherith, that is before Jordan."

Nehemiah 6:9 says, "For they all made us afraid, saying, their hands shall be weaken from the work, that it be not done. Now therefore, O God, strengthen my hands." In Nehemiah, Sanballat sent a letter that said that Nehemiah and the Jews were planning to rebel against the king. They were rebuilding the wall so that Nehemiah could be their king. Nehemiah's prayers to God protected him from the enemies' tricks

God will complete the work that He has started. Don't come down; pass through the waters!

10

Pass through the Waters

To pass means to move or cause to move in a specified direction. It also means a successful completion of a test, examination, or course. *Through* indicates a direction moving from in one side and out of the other side of an opening, continuing in time toward completion of a process or period.

Let's look at Isaiah 43:2:

> When thou passest through the waters, I will be with thee; and through the rivers they shall not overflow thee; when thou walkest through the fire, thou shalt not be burned; neither shall the flame kindle upon thee.

This speaks of Israel's deliverance from Babylonian captivity because of God's love for his people. It is also an expression of God's great love for Israel. As we pass through the water or walk through fire, we will not be destroyed.

God's promise to Israel and to us is to restore a righteous and fruit-bearing remnant among the nations in full demonstration of God's redemptive love.

God will send us to a place in His Word to gain perspective. There at the brook, God will feed us His Word. It is in a hidden place of tears that God will restore us, a place where we couldn't hear the naysayers or the noise. God will hide us in a place away from ourselves to see ourselves and depend on God! It is at the brook, a hidden place where only God can heal, deliver, and instruct, as He did with Elijah, where God gives us His plan, His purpose.

It is at the brook that we pray, see, and declare our enemies saved!

It was at the brook that God took Elijah on to his next journey to Mt. Carmel.

I had to continue on, and even in the drought, God fed me as I journeyed on. God said, "Pass through the waters and just keep swimming!"

Pass through the waters.

Shattered and Splintered Motherhood

The five-month journey of my shattered and splintered motherhood began with me living the meaning of Romans 8:38–39. I was broken into pieces, damaged, crushed, almost destroyed.

It felt like sharp pieces of wood broken off in fractions of my heart.

> For I am convinced that neither death, nor life, nor angels, nor principalities, nor things present, nor things to come, nor powers, nor height, nor depth, nor any other created thing, will be able to separate us from the love of God, which is in Christ Jesus our Lord. (Romans 8:38–39)

Paul said neither death nor life can separate up from the love of God which is in Christ Jesus. One of the greatest places is to live in love and to live in love eternally.

Nothing in this life or eternal life separates the believer from the love of God.

This was proven to me in the death of my son, in divorce, friendships, etc. Nothing in our life experiences, our shortcomings, sufferings, or anything present or things to come can separate us. Nothing in this lifetime, present or future can keep us from His unconditional love!

Paul refers to the height and the depth of any matter, the high place, the recognized level and the complexity and the profundity of thought, the deepness, or anywhere in between.

Absolutely nothing can move, divide, detach, disconnect, sever, rupture, or breach us from *His love*.

Scriptures of Healing for My Son Alex-Michael

Fear thou not; for I [am] with thee (Alex-Michael): be not dismayed; for I [am] thy God: I will strengthen thee (Alex-Michael); yea, I will help thee (Alex-Michael); yea, I will uphold thee (Alex-Michael) with the right hand of my righteousness. (Isaiah 41:10)

Heal me (Alex-Michael), O LORD, and I (Alex-Michael) shall be healed; save me (Alex-Michael), and I (Alex-Michael) shall be saved: for thou [art] my (Alex-Michael's) praise. (Jeremiah 17:14)

Behold, I will bring it health and cure, and I will cure them (Alex-Michael), and will reveal unto them (Alex-Michael) the abundance of peace and truth. (Jeremiah 33:6)

Who his own self bare our sins in his own body on the tree, that we, being dead to sins, should live unto righteousness: by whose stripes ye (Alex-Michael) are healed. (1 Peter 2:24)

But he [was] wounded for our (Alex-Michael's) transgressions, [he was] bruised for our (Alex-Michael's) iniquities: the chastisement of our peace [was] upon him; and with his stripes we (Alex-Michael) are healed. (Isaiah 53:5)

And the prayer of faith shall save the sick, and the Lord shall raise him (Alex-Michael) up; and if he have committed sins, they shall be forgiven him. (James 5:15)

Bless the LORD, O my soul and forget not all his benefits: Who forgiveth all thine iniquities; who healeth all thy (Alex-Michael's) diseases; Who redeemeth thy (Alex-Michael's) life from destruction; who crowneth thee (Alex-Michael) with loving kindness and tender mercies. (Psalm 103:2–4)

Is any sick among you? let him call for the elders of the church; and let them pray over him, anointing him (Alex-Michael) with oil in the name of the Lord. (James 5:14)

Beloved, I wish above all things that thou (Alex-Michael) mayest prosper and be in health, even as thy soul prospereth. (3 John 1:2)

Confess [your] faults one to another, and pray one for another, that ye may be healed. The effectual fervent prayer of a righteous man availeth much. (James 5:16)

The LORD will strengthen him (Alex-Michael) upon the bed of languishing: thou wilt make all his bed in his sickness. (Psalms 41:3)

The Spirit of the Lord spoke to be and said, "You will be famous!"

St. Louis Children's Hospital wanted to do a study that measured newborns' physical reaction to pain.

> St. Louis Post-Dispatch (St. Louis, Missouri), Monday, July 19, 1999

> ...into the ocean in front of the Kennedy family compound Sunday... Alex-Michael Roy Johnson as he sleeps last week in St. Louis Children's Hospital... Physicians for decades thought infants did not feel pain.

My son was featured on the front page of the *St. Louis Post-Dispatch* in July 1999 along with the Kennedy family plane crash story on page one (accessible on https://www.newspapers.com/newspage/142757565/).

ST. LOUIS POST-DISPATCH

Kennedy, passengers are given up for dead

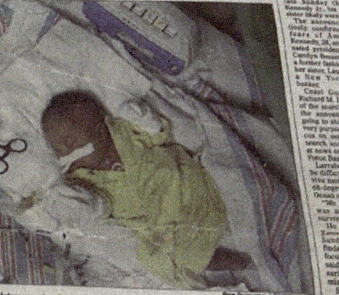
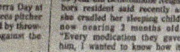
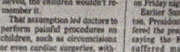

ciation o dis- ay indi- ers.

g recog- an option said the president he associa-

providers have their b whether st interest the heal- promote he said. we might loyee to will be

fficials is is a vote ealth nser- rban

workers and even doctors who are contemplating union affiliations.

Last year, about one-sixth of the nation's 2.6 million registered nurses were covered by collective-bargaining agreements, according to the Bureau of National Affairs, the publisher of many trade magazines. The rate has been increasing in recent years.

Last month, the American Nurses Association voted to create the United American Nurses, a quasi-independent group to handle all of the association's organizing activities. Also last month, the American Medical Association voted to help unionize certain physicians — salaried employees and medical residents — who account for about one-third of U.S. doctors.

"We don't want to make this adversarial," said Karen Prade, a pro-union nurse who has worked at St. John's for 11 years. "If we didn't like the hospital, we would have left a long time ago. We can work together."

the the new contracts must approve ald them for any one of the agreements ot to take effect.

In a taped message to flight attendants last week, union official no Sherry Cooper urged members to k- approve their contract even if they le found it imperfect.

"If you think it's a good start, 3, vote yes," she said, noting that the if new contract would be an improvement over previous contracts because it calls for raises rather than s concessions.

Although some industry observers think TWA can remain viable on its own, others say it should spend the next 18 months looking for a merger or strategic alliance.

Potential partners for TWA were a hot topic last week on Planebusiness.com, a Web site geared toward airline industry employees, investors and aviation buffs.

US Airways was most often mentioned as a partner, followed by America West Airlines and Air-Tran, the carrier formerly known as ValuJet.

US Airways needs a hub in the central United States and more international routes to compete with the industry's other giants — United, American, Delta and Northwest. It also needs to add service in the West to diversify its heavily East Coast-oriented route system.

Morse code, the old language of dots and dashes, has been consumed by the age of bytes. Months after the code was abandoned under international convention for ships in distress, the only private U.S. network of coastal radio stations using Morse has turned off the transmitters. A final ceremonial message was tapped out last week to Washington, where the first such message originated 155 years ago. "Morse code has finally met its match."

FROM NEWS SERVICES

Babies

Study measures infants' reactions to pain

Continued from Page A1

mended that doctors provide pain relievers after circumcisions.

That recommendation, considering an estimated 1.2 million newborn males are circumcised in the United States annually, illustrates how far the medical community has come and still needs to go, Porter said.

"Here we are, in 1999, just now recommending pain management for the most common elective surgery," Porter said.

Parents should get involved in pain management, Porter said. Some questions she recommends:

■ What pain-reduction treatments are available?

■ What are the risks associated with the pain-management techniques?

■ How much experience does the person doing the procedure have with pain-reducing methods?

■ Have the people making the decisions about pain reduction taken into account the infant's weight, sickness and age?

For her study, Porter observed 152 newborns as they underwent procedures ranging from heel sticks to intravenous work. The tests measured heart rates, sleep rates, crying and other physical responses.

The study showed that healthy, full-term infants and children born as many as 28 weeks premature reacted similarly to pain: As procedures went from least invasive — such as checking heart rates with stethoscopes — to most invasive — circumcision — the children's heart rates and fussiness increased.

Researchers also tracked the premature children until they reached full-term age, recording increased agitation and heart rates as they were prepared for other medical proceedings.

Those findings are a good indication that children may grow more sensitive to pain as they age, Porter said.

With regard to current methods of protecting infants from pain, she said the study shows there is "still room for improvement."

Some institutions are taking that cue.

Surgeons at St. Louis Children's Hospital sedated Jackson's son, Alex-Michael Roy Johnson before his operation. He is still in the hospital, recovering from an infection that inflames intestines and can decay them in 24 hours. Doctors removed 75 percent of his small intestine.

Walentik is a pediatric associate professor at Children's Hospital. She said physicians at Cardinal Glennon and St. Mary's Medical Center often use pain-reducing medication for infants even if parents don't ask.

But in an increasing number of cases, parents aren't shying away from questioning.

"Parents are pretty sensitive to the discomfort their children might experience," said Aaron Hamvas, medical director of St. Louis Children's Hospital's neonatal intensive-care unit. He said that sensitivity takes time to develop.

"When a family first comes in, they're just so overwhelmed by having to be in the ICU and the degree of illness," he said.

Still, Walentik said, too often too few parents are asking questions.

"It's not something they think about," she said. "They figure doctors are going to do what's right for them."

18

My beautiful boy was born in the month of May. It was the happiest time of my life. Alex-Michael was his name and he was beautiful. Two eyes, two hands, two feet, ten toes, ten fingers, a beautiful nose, ears, mouth, and the breath of God breathing through his body. Alex-Michael was fine, so I thought, and it was time to go home. My baby boy would have to stay in NICU (neonatal intensive care unit) at the children's hospital in St. Louis, Missouri.

Leaving my son at the hospital, I went home to start my new life without him being there every second. The phones rang. It was the hospital. Not really know what was waiting for me on the other end, I really felt no need to worry. I picked up the phone and a stressful, tormenting, standing-on-the-Word-of-God, prayer warrior journey began.

The doctor on the other end of the phone stated that I needed to get back to the hospital because my baby needed to have an emergency surgery and my signature was needed for authorization. I got there as soon as possible. Alex-Michael was born seven months (twenty-eight weeks) premature, and with that came some internal infections. His intestines were infected, and he had to have a feeding tube in order for him to get nourishment. This would cause my baby to stay in the hospital for five months of his life. That phone called shattered everything in me except my faith and trust in God. That was all I had to stand on and I was not giving that up for anything in this world.

Scriptures of Healing

As Alex-Michael and my journey began on the road of healing, I had to surround myself with healing scriptures on the wall. There was nothing else in view for us but knowing that God was going to heal my son. Throughout this journey, my surroundings was filled with beautiful, healthy babies, and I had produced a life-changing miracle who would forever change my way of thinking. It expanded my prayer life.

I felt empty, as though I had nothing left inside of me. It was like a fall while still being lifted up by God. There was no time to question God about why this happened, but I made sure that I stood on the promises of God and waited on His manifestation.

I waited on my baby to be healed and have the quality of life a baby should have. Alex-Michael's surgery took about an hour, but he was not out of the woods yet. It was a process that we had to journey together, and God remained faithful.

Along the way, Alex-Michael got yellow jaundice and other minor complications that did not help his health situation. I stayed by his side, never leaving him for five months. I began to quote the scriptures that I had placed along the wall and I was constantly in the chapel praying. I wanted to make sure the devil knew that he would have to fight me tooth and nail to make me give up. I did not allow any negativity around my son, and my family was there every step of the way. No matter what it looked like to them, they would continue to stay prayerful and encouraging. Alex-Michael was well loved, and it showed. I quoted scriptures around my son so that the manifestation of God was evident.

Chapel Prayer and the Drum Family

As I continued my journey, there were quite a few families that came through. But there was one family that stood out and that was the Drum family. Nick and Cindy Drum and I connected during my trips to the chapel. As I prayed one day, I felt someone in the chapel and, yes, it was this wonderful family.

The Drum family was a vital instrument while on this journey, and the prayers we joined were a strong support for us all. We were so connected that we started a Bible study that also included nurses and doctors when they had time. The son Justin David Drum died before mine but we stayed connected. I remember praying for them, visiting them in Rochester, Illinois.

I remember the Drums would come up every year to visit the hospital nurses and doctors. I remember God saying, "I'm about to teach you to share…" I said yes, not knowing that of all I prayed for, God gave a double portion to the Drums. In my prayer closet,

I prayed for a big house and seven acres of land, twin children, a renewal! Everything I prayed for God granted to the Drums.

I was thinking about Job and all that God restored for him. Thank You, Jesus, for teaching me to petition to You and share Your blessings. The awareness of getting to know God was evident, and souls were saved. This journey was not just about Alex-Michael but about bringing souls to Christ, even in the midst of my heartache, in the midst of my dark place, and in the midst of my faith walk.

During this season, I was asked to do an interview for the hospital. This interview was in the newspaper and happened to be right below to the JFK story front and center. God has a way of positioning you. I heard the Spirit of the Lord say, "You will be established and succeed!"

The Dreams Kept Coming

Later in this journey, the dreams started to come more vividly, which brought some reality into play. Visions of death were seemingly in every dream, and from that I began to ask God what was really going on. I still stood on the word and the promises of God, but this was beginning to affect me.

You see, this was my little boy, and to think of never having the chance to see his sweet face again, to even think of never being able to smell him, touch him, love on him, or be in his presence was really unimaginable. This baby was mine; God had entrusted him to me. He allowed me to bring forth such a small, precious gift, and to think of losing him, never being able to be a part of his journey in this life, was painful.

I would have loved to see my son graduate from Head Start, elementary, high school, and then college. Yes, a valedictorian with a 4.0 GPA speaking to his class about how he was a walking miracle because of his circumstances. How his mother stayed at the hospital with him for five months and never gave up on him and that she prayed him through. Then off to college, a doctor, a lawyer, or anything he wanted to be. Once he was done with school, he would marry his sweetheart and raise a beautiful family. But before walking down that aisle, they dedicate their lives to God as a family. That was what I would love to see, but that was my dream and not a reality.

I Knew Death Was Coming

The thought of losing my Alex-Michael was more heartbreaking than I could ever imagine. There is no amount of pain that could even be thought of worse than what I endured. You know, when people tell you that they know how you feel, and that it's gonna get better, to you they have no clue.

You don't know the pain a mother feels when she loses her child or is on the brink of having to make a decision to pull the plug. You have no idea of the tears that I have cried, or the tears that my heart cried every second of the day. You don't know my pain when I walk into that hospital room with my baby all plugged in, heart monitors, oxygen machines, IVs, him being helpless and me not able to be helpful. It's tormenting.

No matter how much I stand on the word of God, he's still my flesh and blood. Mary wept for Jesus, and still He understood that she was flesh. Till this day it still hurts; it's branded in my heart. I knew by the dreams that my son was about to be with God sooner than I wanted him to be.

No matter how much I pleaded, prayed, cried, and trusted, God had something totally different from my want and that was His will. I remember while sleeping in the waiting room, making a makeshift bed by putting chairs together, I would doze off and look up at choirs singing sad songs at funerals. I felt in my spirit's closure was near!

The Last Torment

As Alex-Michael's days came close to an end, I began to really feel the hurt, the despair, the agony of having to let my child go forever. Having him in my heart and in my hands are two different things. It's not as easy as people say; it will never be the same without my baby. Outside of God, Alex-Michael was my blessing, and to know that my blessing was at the end was unbearable.

As the days grew near, the doctors updated me on his prognosis daily. The doctors and nurses on each shift were respectful, caring and understanding, except two of them. Two nurses displayed such anger, bitterness, and nastiness to me about my child.

One nurse kept saying to me on a daily basis, "This is it. What are you going to do? You know he at the end. He ain't going to make it." What is that to say to a mother who is losing her child? How do you even fix your mouth to say that? The torment and pain that she brought to that room in saying this to me was unacceptable. The other nurse was mean, harsh, and nasty as well, but this nurse stood out because as the time came and Alex-Michael took his last breath, the longest sound of the machine screeching *beeeeep*, her words to me were "Where is your God now? Where is he now?" All I could say was "He is right here," and I just threw up my hands and began to worship God because I knew my son was with God.

During this time of numbness and hurt, my circle questioned what God was doing. The children thought out loud, "We will never get to play with Alex here." One of my friends said, "I know how you feel," and at that moment, anger set in. I said, "How would you know, you never sat in this seat!" The room grew silent.

Then another spoke loudly, "Just stop crying. Just stop. What do you want from God? He can't do anything. What do you want!" As he screamed continuously, I paused and said for God to resurrect my son. The room really got quiet!

We said goodbye. I knew the angels were with my son on his flight to see Jesus. I knew that my son Alex-Michael was not going to go through any more pain. I knew that my son would be safe, not tormented by this thing we call life. I knew that Alex-Michael would be healed of all his ailments and circumstances. No matter how painful letting go was, I let my baby go to the Father who created us; to the Father who allowed us to be here; to the Father who allowed me to embrace motherhood; to the Father who allowed me to be a mother to Alex-Michael; to a Father who kept Alex-Michael alive for five months; to a Father who allowed my family to love him for the time he was here.

Alex-Michael never left the hospital, but his flight to heaven is believed to be breathtaking. No matter what it looks like, going to be with God will be the brightest day ever. I pray that one day I get to see him again. I just thank God for the experience of knowing what true love really looks and feels like. The breath of God was in my son's body, and that is what love is.

The Homegoing

From beginning to end, the Spirit of the Lord gave me everything regarding preparation. He said, "Turn over, daughter. I'm about to give you instructions that will cost you nothing on earth." He said, "Open the yellow pages, and I will give you an unknown place for you to bury your son." So I took the yellow pages, and it opened to Bellerive Heritage Gardens in Creve Coeur, Missouri. I knew nothing about this place and was not familiar with the county it was in.

I picked up the phone, called the Bellerive Heritage Gardens, and said, "I need your services for my infant son." The lady on the other line was so compassionate; she said, "Where are you?" I said at home; she asked for my address and showed up. She hugged me. I was in awe. She said, "We will do everything free." He just had to be buried in Babyland, where all the babies were. Then she took out a tape recorder and said there would be a computer screen where the names would be displayed in alphabetical order. When I chose his name and once that was brought up, anything I wanted to say will be recorded and played at any visit for memories. The Spirit of the Lord gave me Psalm 91, so I recited it:

> He that dwelleth in the secret place of the most High shall abide under the shadow of the Almighty. I will say of the LORD, He is my refuge and my fortress: my God; in him will I trust. Surely he shall deliver thee from the snare of the fowler, and from the noisome pestilence.
> He shall cover thee with his feathers, and under his wings shalt thou trust: his truth shall be

thy shield and buckler. Thou shalt not be afraid for the terror by night; nor for the arrow that flieth by day; Nor for the pestilence that walketh in darkness; nor for the destruction that wasteth at noonday.

A thousand shall fall at thy side, and ten thousand at thy right hand; but it shall not come nigh thee. Only with thine eyes shalt thou behold and see the reward of the wicked. Because thou hast made the LORD, which is my refuge, even the Most High, thy habitation; There shall no evil befall thee, neither shall any plague come nigh thy dwelling.

For he shall give his angels charge over thee, to keep thee in all thy ways. They shall bear thee up in their hands, lest thou dash thy foot against a stone. Thou shalt tread upon the lion and adder: the young lion and the dragon shalt thou trample under feet. Because he hath set his love upon me, therefore will I deliver him: I will set him on high, because he hath known my name.

He shall call upon me, and I will answer him: I will be with him in trouble; I will deliver him, and honour him. With long life will I satisfy him, and shew him my salvation.

The prayer of protection reigned in my Spirit even today. God reminds us to sit down, to dwell, to remain, to settle in the sense of taking up a homestead or staking out a claim, to process a place and live therein. God provides a covering, a hiding place in Psalm 91; it explains a secret place of the Most High under the defense and protection which I call a place of refuge. Under the shadow of the Almighty God is our fortress, security, and a true and faithful God.

As we dwell with the Lord, He will deliver from the snare of the fowler, which wicked men, fallen angels, and demons set for the righteous. Deliver us from rushing calamity that could have swept everything before it. His "feathers" represent protection and care. He will protect us under His wings, and make a shield and buckle that protects the body and vital parts from the weapons and arrows of the enemy. God protects us no matter what comes!

I submitted pictures. All my bills were paid for five months. It was like when I stayed in prayer before the Lord, He rewarded openly. Our friends from college donated the limo and pick us up from hospital. I thought I would be brave enough to see the last remains, but when I went to see I passed out! I thought if I his mother couldn't view that, I didn't want anyone else to endure it. So we just had pictures and the smallest baby casket you could ever imagine. It changed my life…

My size in clothes went from a sixteen to eight. Spiritually, I was okay. Naturally, people were saying, "We thought we lost you. You are so small." I thought, *I'm on an assignment for the King, and He will restore.* And that He did; my natural weight came back, and every other weight that so easily beset was gone!

The Reassurance from God

I told the Lord I needed to be reassured that Alex-Michael made it in the Lord. As a woman of faith, I still wanted to know. Weeks had passed, and I remember this incident so vividly. I was taking a shower and tears began to roll down my face; as the shower water dripped so did my tears.

My tears seemed to have come as swiftly as the water. I heard the Spirit of the Lord say, "Praise Me! And all of your tears I will bottle up and release joy!" I obeyed the Lord.

"Thank You, Jesus. Thank You, Jesus, for sustaining me! Thank You, Jesus, for keeping me!" Then as my eyes were filled with tears, I raised my hands up and closed my eyes. The Lord said, "Listen."

I could hear Alex-Michael saying, "Mommy, I made it! I made it to heaven!" And on his belly where his affliction was, there was a bright yellow ribbon, and there were other babies running behind him.

He was at the front of the line! Just as we race in a track meet and cross the line as a winner, Alex-Michael was leading and winning. At that moment, I was reassured that he had made it.

Thank You, Jesus!

I fasted for thirty-one days with some days of Absolute and most days just water. I stayed before the face of God, knowing He had the final say on it all. The author and finisher of my faith!

Most days my flesh would be so weak, and then a fresh wind would come from the Word to strengthen me. Many days, I would hear the doctor's report before they even came to meet with me. One of the doctors said, "How did you know about this report I was about to give? This was done at my home. I was working the prognosis from a computer." You see, they had a room where they would gather family members to give a progress report. Well, I would humbly say, "You do everything medically possible, but I will continue to believe the report of the LORD!"

He give life and life more abundantly. The doctors would come to say, "Go to bed. Leave and get some rest!"

Well, the Lord had my family, who are spiritual soldiers, front-line generals, warriors, sergeants, and first privates, on the wall twenty-four seven; my wailing mom, aunts, and clergyman stand in the gap around the clock.

I could remember this one nurse saying, "You pray all the time, too much. Go to bed!"

I said that when the Lord was ready to go to the Father, He did not move but carried out His assignment. So I said to the nurse, "I will stay and pray!" She stormed out. You see, I knew the watch time to pray. I had been listening to a great warrior. There were scriptures all over my son's NICU room, a Bible in his bed, worship music where the power of the Lord's presence abides. I had the twelve o'clock hour, and that's the hour where the witches and warlocks come to try and place something in the atmosphere. But through God, we set a watch of His Word, and He performed miracles of healing and salvation throughout St. Louis Children's Hospital in 1999! There was prayer without ceasing, a mantle of prayer stored up for the Master's use.

Genesis 22:18 says, "And in thy seed shall all nations of the earth be blessed; because thou hast obeyed by voice."

Fragmented and Fractured Ship

Ships are made up of titanium, aluminum, planks, decks, and survivors.

Fragmented of pieces of a ship are like relationships where parts are broken or detached, unfinished, isolated, and incomplete, disunified; relationships that felt the breaking of a bone or the cartilage of the heart. Friendship iron sharpens iron. During this time, I remembered I had not seen my childhood friend for many years. I looked up while in the chapel, and a young lady said, "Angie!" I said, "Wendy Campbell!" She had a uniform on; she worked in the hospital. I thought to myself when the Lord brings someone back, it was for purpose, and that was to sharpen each other in prayer!

So daily she would pray with me and some days she would just show up in the chapel and pray. I would agree with the Word in her for healing. It's one thing to grow up in the natural but another to grow up and find each other in the presence of God and grow like nothing was ever lost!

I meet Wendy in 1972 at Carver Elementary St. Louis, Missouri, where school was from kindergarten to eighth grade. I remember we stood out because we had a two-parent home and we could eat the same lunches, so every day in the seventh and eighth grade we would eat Jack-in-the-Box: two tacos, fries, and a fried apple pie for $2.11 (they don't sell fried pies anymore).

Back then, we were set apart spiritually; we couldn't eat at the same table our classmates ate at. Our parents made too much money for Vital Lunches. So Wendy's big brother would walk us to Jack-in-the-Box for lunch, and we would sit outside pondering why we could not eat with the others waiting for the bell to ring. God had already set us apart for sanctification, and we knew as we know now you can't eat at everyone's table; we were the King's daughters. After graduation in 1980, I didn't see Wendy anymore; she had moved to Germany until 1999, during Alex-Michael's journey at the children's hospital where Wendy worked.

Sound of Trumpet

> Cry aloud, spare not, lift up thy voice like a
> trumpet, and shew my people their transgression,
> and the house of Jacob their sins. (Isaiah 58:1)

This was a command to Isaiah to "cry aloud, spare not, lift up your voice like a trumpet, show My people their sins." God dealt with the nurses and the doctors who had much to say, but what they will remember is that God is faithful and that He was very present during that journey.

God will give us a role of a spiritual watchman among His people, because it is vital to understand the work of God and what is to come. God said to the prophet Ezekiel 3:17, "Son of man, I have made you a watchman for the house of Israel: therefore hear a word from my mouth and give them a warning from me." Watchmen are assigned in our lives to warn and to teach, to overlook the fields from thieves and to guard the harvest. God also will warn us to prepare for battle. The watchman's role is also charged with proclaiming good news about salvation!

Sometimes during our journey, we experience demolition; an overwhelming feeling of defeat, destruction, explosives, bulldozers, wrecking balls. Spiritual maturity starts with the demolition of old habits and the construction of the renewed man.

To float means to move in a motion without sinking; we have to stay spiritually afloat during testing times.

God will rebuild ruins; even the waste places in your life will be restored to a habitual state, and the blessings that should have been enjoyed for many generations will be ours.

We would take shifts crying out to the Lord, "Where are the wailing women?" Jeremiah 9:17 says to call for the women who will fast and cry out to the Lord and be heard from Zion. During our time of prayer, my mother and aunt stayed on their post, crying unto the Lord. The battle cry, day and night. They knew the importance of God's presence and intervention. They sought the Lord intensely and realized that the cause and effect would be the Lord's will.

Repairers of the breach are laborers in the hands of God working to loosen the bonds of wickedness, undo the heavy burdens, and break every yoke that binds mankind in sin. The repairers teach and preach God's holy law of the Spirit of life, love, and liberty. My family means everything to me and God!

Intercessors from every side came to journey with God's purpose for this time. God naturally and spiritually taught us how to be gatekeepers, an attendant of a gate who is employed to control who goes through or who has access.

Wrath over Waiting

When a disobedience, a *no*, causes wrath, just wait on your *yes* from God. I was preparing for a journey of oneness. I had failed to observe the agreement to obey. I had to endure a strong, stern, fierce, and deep consequence of not obeying. An eternal forgiveness I will always ask of the Lord.

I sat in a place of shock and strain. I had to endure such a blow that I didn't think I would ever recover from. A fifteen-year test; a place of trial and pain. As I was preparing, all lights were red, and I still made choices clearly before me. God was so specific; He gave me names and scriptures.

Our time was near to go into prayer; we had a set time to pray, and God would answer.

I remember this so vividly. We decided to go and pray at a sanctuary nearby. The year was 2000. When we got there, we found that Christian Fellowship was having prayer service all week. We were in the right place; we had heard from the Lord where to go. The pastor at the time had the same name and initials that were revealed to me during the trial. The pastor was looking for a wife, and I thought, *Lord, You are giving me a choice.*

Even that place had to endure financial hardship, and the shepherd left the sheep in distress.

My sister and I traveled to a place to seek God at a sanctuary. We both went in separate places and came up with the same scripture. And the same answer of NO.

I even said, "God, if You don't want me to enter in, take me to another place." And God did just that, and I entered in anyway. It was a spirit of NO accountability supported by tradition. You know how we do things wanting to press in and make the Scriptures fit our circumstances.

As I continued, the test got harder and harder. I said, "Lord, if what I'm entering in is a *no*...take me to a place."

The Lord took me out of town for a job training in Dallas, Texas, for three months. During that time, I sought the Lord, but I took a step of disobedience, not knowing that my life of oneness would be filled with disagreement on every matter.

I have endured a spirit of control and pride. I was attending a place of worship that had traditional thinking and traditional support of letting your behavior be of the world: "we have your back *no* matter how it looks."

No accountability.

I began to journey to a place of waiting so that the contract that was signed would please God. Finally, when the test was over, God would say yes to my destination in Him. Even the enemy tried to follow me and set up a distraction where I was headed: a sanctified, Holy Spirit place, a place of deliverance delivering me from the hand of the enemy.

I was in class, and some document came across our bishop's desk that was a character assassination. He said, "Daughter, humility before honor!"

Great leaders know their sheep and their Spirit!

Ravens of Restoration

When we think of a raven, we picture a dark pestilence, an unclean creature. A raven is an excellent flyer with amazing aerial skills. Ravens are effective hunters that use techniques and strategies to devour. Ravens hide in barren places, mountains, and deserts. In this raven-filled place in my journey, I met the meanest creatures, the most hurtful tactics, and character assassinations with no provisions, yet I was fed by God. This journey took me to a hidden place. I was asking myself, could a hidden place become a restored place, a place to reestablish order in my life, a place of health and soundness and vigor?

As I withstood the fiery darts, I experienced Cherith. Cherith means a cutting, a separation, a gorge, a torrent bed, or a winter stream along the Jordan river in the valley. At the brook of Cherith was where Elijah hid and was miraculously fed after the drought of Ahab. That's just like God to send us to the brook to get perspective.

God began to remind me of 1 Kings 17:3: "Get thee hence, and turn thee eastward, and hide thyself by the brook Cherith, that is before Jordan." God rescued Elijah from the fury of Ahab and Jezebel, who, he knew, would seek to destroy him. This was a promise that there would be enough water in the brook Cherith for Elijah to drink, and that ravens would feed Elijah his two daily meals.

God sent Elijah to this remote and retired place where he was concealed so that neither friends nor foes might know where he was. A dry place, a valley.

God chose a dark bird to feed Elijah. The ravens were appointed to bring him meat and did so. Sometimes God will allow our foes to feed us, and we must trust it. God could have sent angels to minister to him; but He chose to show that He can serve His own purposes by the meanest creatures to be the mightiest. The natural supply of water failed but the miraculous supply of food, made sure to him by promise, failed not.

But there is a river which makes glad the city of God that never runs dry, a well of water that springs up to eternal life. Lord, give us that living water!

God commanded the ravens to feed Elijah. The ravens could have eaten him, just as we might have been eaten when we encounter circumstances, but at the brook, God fed me with His Word. In my hidden place of tears, God restored me. God will hide us in a place away from ourselves to see ourselves. Depend on God! I had to run and hide myself in God; I was called to a place of solitude.

I was in a place of separation naturally and spiritually where I could not be useful for God. So I had to sit quietly for Him. God will feed you according to His promises. I had to trust God for daily bread, for provision, and for purpose!

The ravens that tried to destroy my life were appointed to bring me meat.

I remember while on my knees praying, my mother said, "I know you are shut in, but there is a call for you that seems to be urgent." I asked God, "Should I answer, and should I go?" I received a yes.

I went and I received an abundance of money that had been stored up by the ravens looking for me.

I had no supply of food, no shelter, walked away from every material thing. But God faileth not!

Sometimes we have to lose what we think we need most.

Here the prophet Elijah had to pass through the waters. First Kings 17:6 says, "And the ravens brought him bread and flesh in the morning and the bread and flesh in the evening and he drank of the brook." Elijah got to the brook and had plenty of water to drink. Just as God had said, every morning and every night He sent ravens with bread and meat for Elijah to eat. The prophet had to trust God and be fed by unclean raven. When you obey the Lord, He will feed you. Just *pass through the waters*!

At the journey to restoration, God healed, delivered, instructed, and fed me. As I traveled, I was brought to a wholesome place to pray, see, and declared my enemies saved! At the brook, it always takes the water to restore us, refresh us, renew us, and sustain us.

This journey was designed just for me; heavy rains and a storm that almost washed up on the shore. I could get my bearings or pull over. The speed of the current was massive, and I thought it would overtake me. I was reminded of Isaiah 43:2.

> When thou passes through the waters, I will
> be with thee; and through the rivers they shall
> not overflow thee; when thou walkest through
> the for, thou shall not be burned; neither shall
> the flame kindle upon thee.

Twelve things that God did for Israel and that He will do for us:

1. Be with us when we go through the waters.
2. Keep the waters from overflowing us.
3. Keep us from being burned when in the fire. (Fire and water are often mentioned in Scripture to denote calamity because one overwhelms and the other consumes.)
4. Punish others in preference to us.
5. Gather us from all lands.
6. Protect us and work for us; and no man can hinder Him.
7. Punish our enemies.
8. Destroy our enemies forever.
9. Make abundant waters for us to use, even in the desert.
10. Make a way for us in the wilderness.
11. Blot out our transgressions.
12. Remember our sins no more.

God led me to pray through firepower ministries, which equip you for spiritual warfare. Firepower is a military capability to target and direct the enemy by force. Firepower prayers involve the whole range of potential spiritual weapons. I had to be kingdom-minded and I had to be in place of no gaps, no breaks, no interruptions, and no disruptions so that I could be restored and mended.

> That in blessing I will bless thee, and in multiplying I will multiply they seed as the stars of the heaven, and as the sand which is upon the seashore; and they seed shall possess the gate of his enemies. (Genesis 22:17–18)

The Lord commanded a fivefold blessing for threefold obedience:

> I will bless you.
> I will multiply you as numerously as the stars.
> I will multiply you as numerously as the sand.
> Your seed shall be victorious.
> All nations will be blessed through your seed!

I'm still on this journey, hearing God say, "I will restore such a one!" He brought me back into existence and reestablished me for the Master's use from the torn and broken places, all for His purpose.

> And we know that all things works together for good to them that love God, to them who have been called according to his purpose! (Romans 8:28)

We know while all things are working, God's providence is working on behalf of them who love God and who walk obediently according to His purpose.

The following poem was dedicated to me by a coworker from a place at work where we prayed and celebrated Jesus.

Broken for Purpose
(by Annie Thompson)

We are not just the sum of elegance and beauty
We are ladies of virtue that have been called to duty
And in order for God to use us to the fullest extent
We had to be *broken* to discover our strength

He never told us there would be no pain
Just that it gets better with time and the more wisdom we gain
So as we stand at the window of our souls looking out while others look in
Our mission is to enter into a relationship that will never end

For He's assured us He'll help us win the battles we fight
And that He'll be with us in our darkest days and our darkest nights
So we can find that peaceful place within us and dare to dream
Knowing that we are safe and our souls have been redeemed

So don't worry about the essence of who you are or where the pieces fall
Because it's not them that keep us together; it's He who makes us whole
Just have faith in the things not seen as He holds on to you
And await the moment when He will make us all brand-new

Until then, continue to walk in your excel-
lence, you ladies of virtue
And don't forget whose you are; to thine
own self be true
And just like the elegance of Waterford
crystal
Let your inner beauty shine through

Because the *brokenness* doesn't define us; it's
only there to make us strong
Afresh with new purpose; in our hearts a
new song
And the *brokenness* inside us is the price we
have to pay
For we were broken for His purpose, He
planned it and He paved the way.

The song etched in my heart is STILL I SAY THANK YOU by
Smokie Norful.

For everything that we have endured as God's yielded vessels to
get to where I am in Christ, I'm humbled. My tears have brought on
my greatest victories; they watered the land for God.

God will never forget our investment. Through God's continued fulfillment of purpose in my life, my family's life, my son's life,
people will be saved and restored. I thank God for the privilege to
dedicate my life to counsel and restore family and for the preserva-
tion of this privilege.

Notes

Notes

Notes

Notes

Notes

Notes

_____

_____

_____

_____

_____

_____

_____

_____

_____

_____

_____

_____

Notes

About the Author

Angela Jackson also known as Yielding Vessel is the author of *Broken for Purpose*, a book that shifts your mindset on what it means to be broken for greatness and realize your life's purpose. She is a native of St. Louis and mother of a son in his first year of college. Yielding Vessel has over twenty years in corporate America and has founded a nonprofit to encourage women and youth. She is a minister and praise dance leader at her church. She is a native of St. Louis, Missouri, and holds a BS in marketing and a master's in leadership development. She is currently studying for her second master's in counseling.